BAHAMAS

Nassau - Paradise Island - Freeport - Family Islands

Great Inagua - Mayaguana - Crooked Island - Acklins Island

BONECHI & LMH PUBLISHING LTD

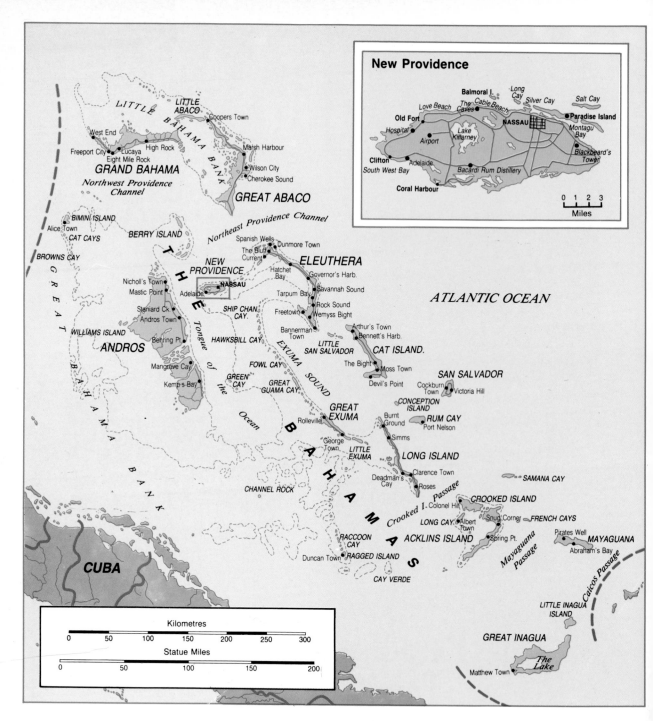

© Copyright by CASA EDITRICE BONECHI, Via Cairoli 18/b - 50131 Firenze - Tel +39 055576841 - Fax +39 0555000766
E-mail: bonechi@bonechi.it   Internet: www.bonechi.it

New York Address:
98 Thompson Street # 38 - New York, N.Y. 10012
Tel.: (212) 343-9235 - Fax: (212) 625-9636 - E-mail: bonechinyc@aol.com

Texts by: Vanni Berti, Mike Henry-LMH Publishing Ltd, Giovanna Magi, Cristiana Pace.
Text pages 59/60 by Bruno Foggi. *Text page 63 by* Leonardo Olmi.

Project and editorial conception: Casa Editrice Bonechi; *Publication Manager:* Monica Bonechi.
Cover: Manuela Ranfagni; *Graphic design, lay-out and make-up:* Vanni Berti, Manuela Ranfagni; *Editing:* Anna Baldini

Printed in Italy by Centro Stampa Editoriale Bonechi.

ISBN 88-476-0395-1

* * *

INTRODUCTION

*T*he Bahamas is a country to be seen and experienced. Its geographical position has allowed it to play a significant role in world history, as a stopping place for pirates, a resting place for slave ships, a haven for gun runners, a hideout for German submarines during the two world wars, and later a port of exchange for drugs.
But the aim of the Bahamas is not to take into consideration only these things of which they are fully aware. It is instead to find comfort and security in their families and in the rich heritage which is theirs, and using all this continue to develop powerful institutions which seem to grow stronger as time passes.
Like most of its Caribbean counterparts, the Bahamas possess a dazzling array of tropical flowers, all of which add their own varied splashes of colour.
Around the 700 islands, tiny caps, and nameless rocks, the sea of many shades seems to ebb and flow like a quilt in the wind. On Inagua the flamingoes pose and preen. The streets of Freeport bring one close to what could be called middle America, and the unexpected colours of the poincianna tree seem to haunt the eye and tantalize the senses with fragance.
Although there are not great distances between the islands, each in its own way is unique, from the mud flats of the Andros islands to the fish-laden waters of the Berry Islands.

Bahamas, the beach and vegetation.

History

EARLY DAYS

"There is no better people in the world" wrote Columbus of the **Lucayans** who welcomed him when he landed on October 12th 1492. The Lucayans inhabited most of what we now call the Bahamas and had done so for over 500 years. A peaceful, graceful, and docile people. They used to sleep on a net stretched out between two stakes which they called "hamac" and which Columbus thought was so comfortable that he got his crew to make use of it, and so introduced the hammock to the western world. They lived primarily off the sea and were skilful fishermen, and were able to paddle expertly over the long and dangerous distance between islands in long ocean – going canoes. Though the Lucayans possessed spears, bows and arrows. They were not warriors and very often came off worse during the deadly attacks of the cannabalistic Caribs; however, the attacks were a mere trifle compared with what was to come after that fateful October. As Columbus reported, "They are ingenious and generous with all they have, they invite you to share it and show that their hearts are full of love." Then the Spaniards, in their eager search for gold on the island of Hispaniola (now Haiti and Dominican Republic), took the Lucayans along with them as indispensable labour, and within 25 years the Lucayans – once some 40,000 strong – had all disappeared and the Bahamas was left depopulated by its cruel and casual conquerors.

SPANISH DAYS SETTLEMENT

After the Spaniards had deprived the native tribe of their islands, they found no reason to go there other than as a port of call for the galleons laden with

treasures on their way back to Spain; one exception was Ponce de Leon who sailed around the islands in search of the legendary "fountain of youth". He did not find the fountain, but, by way of compensation he discovered Florida. Strange as it may be, the islands did not belong to anyone, and seafarers of different nationalities (Spanish, British, French and Dutch) sailed around them until the British suddenly realised how important the Bahamas were, and so in 1629 Charles I granted the islands to his Attorney General.

BRITISH DAYS

The Bahamas then came under the proprietary rights of Sir Robert Heath; but to claim the 600 mile wide island group as one's own was one thing, to prove it was another; and so 4 years later France gathered several of the already granted islands in a grant to King Charles I's favourite, who was caught in a Puritan revolt and lost his head. As a result of this dispute the Bahamas gained its first permanent settlement at **Eleuthera** when a ship called "The William" struck a reef off the north coast of the island; this group of Puritans were led by William Sayle, a former Governor of Bermuda. This attempt at settlement at first made little progress, as life on Eleuthera was very hard, and despite the support of other Puritans, by 1657 Sayle himself had returned to Bermuda. The colony kept growing nevertheless, attracting new Puritans and freed slaves. It was during this period that Sayle, on one of his tireless voyages on behalf of the colony, sought refuge from a fierce storm in a particularly fine harbour. The island which residents named in his honour is today known as **New Providence**. Its main city is of course **Nassau**, the economical and political capital of the Bahamas.

A NEW COLONY

At the same time as the Puritan adventurers were fighting their battles against unyielding elements, Charles III, now restored to the British throne, was again granting proprietary rights to the Bahamas, this time to several powerful lords.
These lords appointed a governor to run the settlement that was growing into Nassau. New Providence continued to grow throughout the 17th century, paying host to such colourful characters as the pirate Blackbeard and Ann Bonney and giving rise to the legalization of piracy, then called Privateering, which was authorized by the government; all of this led to the Spaniards sacking Nassau, and on four occasions, burning it to the ground. In spite of this Nassau, like a phoenix, rose again after each attack, attracting once again its fair share of criminals and solid citizens; but the lord proprietors felt the need for a new direction and sent Woodes Rogers as the Royal Governor of a colony, now under the direct control of the Crown. He had strict instructions to restore law and order.

Sunset amid the palms on one of the many beaches of the Bahamas.

THE EIGHTEENTH CENTURY

Woodes arrived in New Providence and immediately set about his task using both skill and wisdom. He offered pardons to pirates while at the same time carrying out public hangings of those who failed to accept his authority.His description of his tenure became the motto of the nation: "Expulsis Piratis - Restituta Commercia" *(He expelled the pirates and restored commerce).* In 1729, Woodes Rogers called together an assembly of the Bahamas. Thereafter it rarely missed a session making it one of the longest lasting assemblies in the New World. While the assembly lasted, it selfishly represented its own narrow interests, opposing governor after governor (taking a firm position against many Crown reforms and the influence and power of the 20th-century liberals).

The thirteen colonies that at that time existed declared a rebellion against Britain in the 1770s, which resulted in 1776 in the American invasion of Nassau, which lasted only two weeks. This was again repeated in 1778, but it was the Spaniards who conquered Nassau in 1782 bringing the Bahamas under a foreign flag for almost a year; this was the only real interruption by a foreign country in the islands' long allegiance to Britain. The British recovered the Bahamas at the treaty of Versailles in 1783 when the thirteen colonies gained their freedom. Britain had traded Florida for the Bahamas. American loyalists arrived during the next ten years introducing slavery and the growth of cotton, which subsequently failed.

EMANCIPATION AND AFTER

Slavery as an institution was doomed in the British Empire, so in 1772 its practice was considered against the law in the home country and in 1807 the slave trade was prohibited throughout all British possessions. By 1834 all Blacks had been emancipated.

The beginning of the 19th century marked the end of the romantic period and by the middle of this century, especially in the period 1861-1865, the Bahamas enjoyed a boom that would not be equalled for some sixty years.

The American civil war led to unparalleled growth, it gave rise to a building boom of warehouses, piers, houses, and stores in the streets along the harbour. Out islanders crowded into Nassau. When the American civil war came to an end at Appomatox in 1865, the effect was quickly felt in the Bahamas where it left a country with a great deal of manpower controlled by a powerful few.

As the century wore on, many Bahamians became immigrant labourers by moving to the United States. When the First World War broke out in 1914, the Bahamians volunteered for both the Canadian and the British West Indies forces thus strengthening even further their ties with the British.

A NEW CENTURY

The concept of the tourist is an old one in the Western hemisphere but it didn't acquire true meaning in the Bahamas until the end of the 19th century. Wealthy people's custom to leave cold climates for warmer ones was becoming fast established, and so the boom of the tourist industry in Florida was followed also in the Bahamas, when Henry Flager built a new hotel in Nassau, where before they had only catered for the established old style luxury hotels such as the Royal Victoria. However, it took Sir Stafford Sands, a man of rare abiltity to see the real potential, when in the 1950's he set up a development Board (now known as the Ministry of Tourism) to promote holidays in the Bahamas for North Americans. After this it became a primary vacation spot, and modern banking laws were made creating a tax haven in the Bahamas. This created huge numbers of jobs, and a professional middle class. At the peak of this success the end was nearing for what was known as the Bay Street Boys, the affluent, mostly white power brokers who had run the Bahamas for most of the 20th century. In the late 1950's and early 1960's public scrutiny gave rise to modern day party politics resulting in the formation of the Progressive Liberal Party (P.L.P.) and the blacks had a say in the matter for the first time, as before this they had little or no say in the affairs of government. It was now clear to everyone except the Bay Street Boys, who formed the United Bahamian Party (U.B.P.), that a big change was taking place in the Bahamas. The taxi strike that accompanied the opening of the new International Airport was the catalyst which soon spread to other industries and showed the strength of black labour, in alliance with the P.L.P. rather than the U.B.P.

Following this, a new constitution was drawn up in 1963 in London and it dissolved and weakened white assembly power and turned the Legislature into a more representative body of both blacks and whites. The U.B.P., led by Roland Symonette, beat back the P.L.P. in nationwide elections, which led to the P.L.P. boycott of the proceedings in Parliament where Lynden Pindling led a practised form of disobedience in the assembly, refusing to obey the Speaker's dictates. The next elections in 1967 saw the election of two independent candidates who subsequently threw in their seats with the P.L.P. and Lynden Pindling's party triumphed over the U.B.P. and came to power. A new constitution was again established and Britain gave all the signs that it was out of the colonial arena and the Bahamas could have its independence whenever it desired; so in 1972, when new elections took place, the P.L.P. overthrew the F.N.M. which had come to replace the old U.B.P. The F.N.M. gracefully accepted the inevitable and joined the negotiating team in creating the First Independent Constitution.

A NEW NATION

After ruling for 19 years, the P.L.P. lost the 1991 General Elections to the restored F.N.M. led by Hubert Ingraham, the now Prime Minister and a former protégé of Lynden Pindling.
Tainted by an air of corruption and drug-associated rumors, the early years of the new F.N.M. Government saw the investigation of the past P.L.P. administration and much exposure of an administration that apparently had been overcome with too much power.
*The F.N.M. Government, having restored the stability of the country, was returned to Government in 1996 and immediately focused its attention on stemming the economic decline, especially in tourism, the mainstay of the economy. The Government invited in major developers from Jamaica and strangely enough South Africa. The C.E.O.s of these Jamaican companies (namely, Gordon "Butch" Stewart of Sandals, John Issa of Superclubs, and Chris Blackwell of Island Records fame) saw to the expanded development of the **Cable Beach**-Compass Point area and Sol Krezner of Sun International bought Paradise Island to develop the 800 million dollar **Atlantis** resort of 2400 rooms, the largest in the Caribbean. The Government also built a new and additional access bridge allowing traffic to flow in and out of "Paradise". As the new millennium approaches, the future for this chain of 700 islands seems firmly rooted in its tried and proven democracy, and the **Family Islands** of Abaco, Eleuthera, Exuma Bimini, and San Salvador will increasingly attract the eye of the investor. Although the road ahead is challenging, one has to leave the Island fully confident that the Bahamas will make it. That the Bahamas will increasingly make its mark in sports on the world stage will be self evident in the achievement of its athletes, while its citizens stridently shout its motto "Forward, Upward, Onward Together."*

An image of Compass Point.

New Providence

For centuries, the island of New Providence has been the most important centre of the Bahamas, despite its small size. **Nassau**, the capital, is the queen of the archipelago, the magnet that draws tourists, and the pride of the Bahamians themselves, who immigrate here from the other islands in search of work. For this reason, New Providence is the most densely-populated of the Bahama islands, and it is here, more than anywhere else, that the contrasts emerge: alongside the showy modernity of Nassau one finds historical artifacts such as the old British fortifications and the ancient African settlements, all surrounded by splendid beaches and elegant estates. Contrasts also exist between the capital, a modern city in which the rhythm is truly "metropolitan", and the island's other centres, such as the town of Adelaide, where life plays out to quiet rhythms and the ambience is "old-fashioned". The town was founded in 1831 by the governor James Carmichael Smyth and named for the wife of King William IV. Its first inhabitants were 157 African slaves who had been "commandeered" by the English (who had abolished slavery) from a Portuguese ship and brought to the island: as the slaves set foot on British soil they became free men. They were transferred from the capital to Adelaide, and charged with building that which was to become their village and cultivating the surrounding land.

It is not only in the cities that one notices the island's accentuated contrasts, but in the landscape as well. New Providence is for the most part a flat island, with only one string of hills; the eastern coast is almost all rocky, the southern coast is marshy in places, and the western part of the island is covered with forests. Alongside all of this are the perfect days and the starry nights of **Paradise Island**, a preferred stopping-place for visitors, whether they be rich sheiks or normal tourists from all over the world.

In short, in this small scrap of land banks and finance companies, hotels and luxury villas, colonial buildings and fortifications, suburban communities, and fabulous beaches all unite to create a pleasing patchwork that detracts nothing from the elemental charm and the beguiling atmosphere of the island.

Nassau, *the coast line.*

NASSAU

View from above Nassau's *harbour.*

In the past, for most of the world the Bahamas was Nassau, the commercial centre of the country, located on the island of New Providence. The contrast between **Downtown** Nassau with its colonial architectural heritage and charm and the much humbler and poorer areas over the hill is noticeable to the visitor.

Originally Nassau was known as Charlestown, but took its present name in honour of the Prince of Orange-Nassau, who became William III of England. Nassau grew from some 160 houses in 1695 to the modern metropolis that it is today. In the 1740s, Fort Nassau was renovated and Fort Montagu built. Expansion and development grew during William Shirley's governorship and still today Shirley Street honours his name, but it was the loyalists fleeing from the newly independent states who transformed the city, bringing with them the architectural style of the southern United States. The development of such local industries as sponge, pineapples, and sisal were the backbone of the late 19th century until bootlegging took over in the early 20th century, paralleled at the same time by Nassau's entry into the worldwide banking and international business and complimented of course by the phenomenon of tourism in the middle of the 20th century. The Bahamas, which is sometimes called "the Switzerland of the West" because of its strict secrecy laws, has no income tax, sales tax, capital gains tax, estate tax, or inheritance tax. The nation's stable government and economy and its proximity to the United States add to making it a most attractive area for investors from all over the world.

Parliament Square *with its statue of* Queen Victoria *and the colonial facade of* Churchill building.

PARLIAMENT SQUARE AND PUBLIC BUILDINGS

Built between 1805 and 1813, the three buildings originally housed the post office, Legislative Council, Court Room, Treasury, the Assembly House. At that time they also overlooked the harbour, which extended as far as Bay Street. The buildings were based on Governor Tyron's Palace in New Bern, the ancient capital of North Carolina. The building in the middle now houses the Senate Chamber, the Supreme Court, and the government publication office, while the western building still houses the Assembly House, Parliament, which still meets under the watchful eye of the **statue of Queen Victoria**. On the opposite side is Rawson Square where the bust of Sir Milo Butler, the first Bahamian Governor General of independent Bahamas, stands. It was sculpted by William Johnson of Little Harbour Abaco. The **Churchill building**, which houses the Prime Minister's office, the Treasury, and the Ministry of Finance, overlooks this recently designed square, which is a constant hum of frenetic movement of crowds of visitors who make Nassau the Mecca of enjoyment as if to emphasize that it is better in the Bahamas.

The flight of steps leading to Government House *and the statue of* Cristopher Columbus.

The statue erected in honour of Christopher Columbus, *the discoverer of these islands.*

GOVERNMENT HOUSE

It was to this house that the Duke and Duchess of Windsor were sent by the Prime Minister, Winston Churchill, during World War II, as Governor and Commander in Chief of the Bahamas. As expected and fairly representational of their approach to life, the Duke and Duchess brought style and elegance and a certain fashion that had not been seen before in the Bahamas. Government House was built in 1801 and is the official residence of the Governor General, the Queen's representative in the Bahamas. This is a pink and white neo-classical mansion located on Mt. Fitzwilliam. There is a **statue of Christopher Columbus** on the front steps. This was imported by Sir James Carmichael Smyth, who presented it to the colony. It was of course the residence of Sir Milo Butler, the first Bahamian Governor General of the newly independent Bahamas; and of his successor Sir Gerald Cash, and now of the present Governor General Sir Orville Turnquest.

An image of Government House.

THE CHANGING OF THE GUARD

*O*ne of the most memorable and picturesque sights for all visitors is without doubt the Royal Bahamian Police, who are splendid in their bright uniforms, enhanced by their contrasting leopard skins which complement the precision and timing with which they carry out the Changing of the Guard.

Two stages of the Changing of the Guard Ceremony.

NASSAU PUBLIC LIBRARY

The Nassau Public Library, next to the more modern Supreme Court building, was built as a prison between 1798 and 1800. It was converted to contain the Nassau public library collection in 1873. Its exterior has recently been renovated. Inside this quaint building can be found the best collection of books on the history of the Bahamas. Its collection of prints and maps, and old photographs goes together with a fine newspaper and stamp collection. Its artifacts include a small collection of Arawak remains, including a Lucayan skull, stone Celts, and a stone Duho (an Indian ceremonial stool).

The exterior of Nassau's Public Library.

"Gourmet Dish" by Chef Phillip Bethel.

BAHAMIAN FOOD

The cooking of the Caribbean is an eclectic blend of European, Indian, Chinese, and African influences. Herbs and spices, tropical vegetables, spanking-fresh seafood, well seasoned meats and poultry and exotic fruits are all binding ingredients of the Caribbean cuisine, which in the Bahamas becomes more adventurous, tastier, and even spicier. Bahamian national food is conch (pronounced "conk"), a large mollusk prepared raw in a salad, frittered, or cracked and served with hot sauce. Peas 'n' rice are a staple, fried chicken and chicken souse are very popular, and "mutton", which can be goat or lamb usually curried, is often on menus together with grouper and spiny lobster or crawfish. The islands' best known fruits are papaya, which is called pawpaw, mango, sapodilla, and sugar apple, and their best sweets are coconut tart, guava duff, sugar bananas, and rum-raisin ice cream.

Bay Street, *former site of the old British Colonial Hotel, now being fully refurbished to become proud member of the Hilton family chain.*

BAY STREET

Bay Street (or the Strand as it was once called) is the oldest street in Nassau and surrounded the town along the harbour. It was Bay Street that gave legitimacy and illegitimacy to the now famous Bay Street Boys, that band of powerful merchants and lawyers who controlled the country until independence. Today Bay Street is still the centre of the commercial area with beautiful Bahamian women in elegant clothes and men in their fashionable three-piece suits and monogrammed shirts. The Bahamian policemen and policewomen are there too, directing the traffic, giving parking tickets or escorting persons awaiting trial at the Magistrates Court situated in Rawson Square. As every new day dawns Bay Street gives rise to a caucophony of noises: the

hooting of car horns, police whistles, laughter, fruit and vegetable vendors, straw workers hawking their wares, the clatter of the horse and carriage all blending with the roar of motor bikes, all struggling to find a space in the crowded street and yet seeming to make space for the crowds of day trippers from the many pleasure cruisers arriving at Prince George Docks. The holiday-makers are equipped with cameras and wear gay coloured shirts advertising that it is better in the Bahamas. Reggae, Soca, and American rock music blare out from car stereos or those carried by young men, some walking about like Zombies caught up in the net of both drug pushers and users. This typically modern scene has resulted in the change from a

quaint elegant fishing village to a fast moving, razzmatazz U.S.-like city with its annual celebration from 26th December through 1st January in Bay Street. This is Junkanoo, the African festival of dance accompanied by the Goombay drums made of goat skin. On Boxing Day and New Year's Day you can hear the sound of cowbells, bugles, horns, whistles, and conch shells when the Bahamas have their parade down Bay Street.

On these pages, two coloured "horse & carriage" take tourists along Bay Street in Nassau where any occasion is right to have parades and hear some music; below, corner of Bay Street and Charlotte Street.

On these pages, some views of the Straw Market. *The lively straw market has become a must for people who stop at Nassau even for a few hours.*

STRAW MARKET

The new Straw Market is built on the site of what once was the Public Market in Bay Street. It was originally built in 1901 and destroyed by fire in 1974. The new Straw Market is part of the complex which also houses the new Ministry of Tourism offices. Here in this lively and bustling market there are mainly women selling their straw work, T-shirts, native jewellery, and wooden carvings. It depends mainly on tourists. With typical Bahamian dexterity, the thatch palm has been converted into a pot-pourri of baskets, hats, mats and dolls.

The increasing migration of Haitians has led to the development of the art of sculpting, which can be paralleled to Bahamian painting of which Amos Ferguson is among the leading exponents.

On these pages, three views of the famous Queen's Staircase with sellers of local crafts crowding along the shady avenue.

THE QUEEN'S STAIRCASE

The Queen's Staircase is located just past Princess Margaret Hospital, so named in honour of the visit in 1955. These sixty-six steps lead to Fort Fincastle and are said to have been cut in the sandstone cliffs by slaves in 1793 to provide access from the town to the fort. The road, in the shade of palms, leading to the steps is a large coloured open-air shop where stalls display typical clothes and local crafts. Today, a climb up these steps will provide a panoramic view of the island.

The cannons of Fort Fincastle *still seem to watch over the coast to protect the city, which stretches out at the foot of the fort.*

This 70 meter high tank tower, located at the top of Bennet's Hill *next to* Fort Fincastle, *offers a beautiful view of the port and city as far as* Paradise Island.

FORT FINCASTLE

Y ou can get to the top of this fort, situated on **Bennet's Hill**, by going up the sixty-six steps of the Queen's Staircase, built by Lord Dunmore in the shape of a paddle steamer. Fort Fincastle overlooks Nassau to guard "all the town and the road eastward where the enemy would probably carry out a landing." Nassau, however, was never attacked after the construction of the fort in 1793. The fort served as a lighthouse until 1817 and was subsequently used as a signal tower. From this vantage point one can see the port of Nassau teeming with its cruise ships and in the distance the new Paradise Island bridge and the island itself.

Some views of Fort Charlotte. *The main part of the fort was completed in 1789. The central bastion,* Fort Stanley, *and the part on the far west side,* Fort D'Arcy, *were added later.*

FORT CHARLOTTE

This huge hulking stone structure dominates Nassau harbour with its massive cannons. It was built in 1787 by the Earl of Dunmore, the Governor of the Bahamas from 1787 to 1796; it was he who named it after George III's wife. The fort contains labyrinths of stone rooms and a dungeon, and was the site of the raising of the flag of the newly independent Bahamas in 1973. It was intended to defend the city against attacks from the west of the island, but notwithstanding its 42 mighty cannons never has a shot been fired in anger. It stands today as a historic monument on 100 acres (40 hectares) which Dunmore reserved as public land.

FORT MONTAGU

This fort was built in 1742 on a point to the Eastern entrance to New Providence harbour. It is the island's third fort and also the oldest, it was built to defend Nassau, but did so unsuccessfully, as in 1776 it failed to drive back the Americans and the Spanish in 1782, when they captured New Providence. Today the fort and the adjacent beach are popular attractions for locals and visitors alike.

Two views of Fort Montagu, *the island's third fort.*

BLACKBEARD'S TOWER

Close to East Bay is Blackbeard's Tower, an ancient fortification believed to have been used by Edward Teach or "Blackbeard", the notorius pirate who frequented Bahamian waters in the 16th and 17th centuries. It is said that Blackbeard used the tower as a lookout for passing ships; which he would attack and plunder. During his reign there was no other pirate more feared.

The building which is said to have been the vengeance tower for the famous pirate Blackbeard. The particular conformation of these coast lines with their countless bays, natural ports, and canals enabled numerous pirates and buccaneers of the past to take refuge and use them as a starting point for their raids.

In the Ardastra Gardens one can find, just like in a magic Eden, birds of all colours and especially beautiful pink flamingoes.

ARDASTRA GARDENS

Just outside Nassau, is the Ardastra Gardens, a kind of small and aberrant zoo, offering one of the most beautiful shows on the island: a parade of about fifty pink flamingoes, trained perfectly; they move together with great elegance at their trainer's instructions. Here is also housed a lonely lion, looking a little out of place among the stately flamingoes that strut and preen. It is difficult to believe that man once enjoyed eating these birds, which were described as having an exquisite taste. The **flamingo** was recently declared the national bird of the Bahamas and appears on the *National coat of arms*: in the centre there is Columbus' caraval, on the left the blue marlin, and on the right the elegant flamingo resting its claw on the ship. In these gardens we can also find such exotic birds as pheasants, peacocks, spoonbills and other waterbirds, all of which parade past the observer in natural splendour.

Nassau fishermen bring in the day's catch. Nowadays fishermen catch fish all the year round, mainly to supply local needs.

PORT

Prince George Wharf and harbour and the Port of Nassau were very important to the development of the city of Nassau. Once the harbour extended as far as Bay Street, but it grew so much in importance and became so busy in the late 1920's, during the prohibition period, that the harbour had to be dredged to 25 feet (8 metres) to cope with increased shipping. The wharf was built and named after Prince George, the Duke of Kent, to commemorate his visit in 1927. Passengers arriving in New Providence by ship all land here and cruise ships make daily calls. The largest yacht in the world, the HSM Britannia (Her Majesty Queen Elizabeth II's yacht) has docked here many times and no doubt like many others has enjoyed the beauty of the Bahamian sunset.

Everyday the beautiful cruisers, which are increasing in number, dock alongside Nassau's Prince George Pier.

PARADISE BRIDGE TO ATLANTIS

Up until 1998 the only link between Nassau and Paradise Island was the 1500 feet (460 metre) Paradise Island Bridge, a smooth concrete bridge that arches over the harbour, at the foot of which there is a toll gate for the payment of the tolls. Pay your toll and enter paradise!
Then in stepped Sol Krezner and a new government and with the advent of Atlantis a new bridge was added, making it easier to return and enter paradise.

QUEEN CONCH

Many of the smaller fishing vessels, especially Bahamian work boat sloops, are actively engaged in catching conch ("conching"). The conch, famous for its beautiful pink shell and for its beautiful and strange shape, has long been a vital and staple part of the Bahamian diet. Its different uses are amply illustrated in the various ways it is eaten, from raw in salads, smoked and cooked in fritters, chowder, as cracked conch, cracked burgers, soused, conch and rice, or stewed and steamed, to name but few of the varied ways in which the Bahamian has tried to underline its well known reputation as an aphrodisiac, a fact all Bahamian men will swear by.

With very rapid and skilful movements the fishermen take out conch from its shell. The "conch" can be enjoyed in numerous and very tasty dishes.

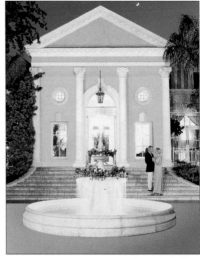

CABLE BEACH

This area, named thus in 1892, when it was the site of the first cable communication with the outside world, has developed into the Riviera of the Bahamas. In 1954 the doors of the Emerald Beach Hotel opened, issuing in the entrance of the first air conditioned hotel.

The old Emerald Beach Hotel is now the site of the four tower complex of gleaming glass and pastel colours and boasts the Radisson Crystal Palace Hotel and Casino, with a complex of shops and an entertainment centre.

The fantastic stretch of white sand has attracted the recent all inclusive giants from Jamaica, as it now boasts Butch Stewart's Sandals Royal Bahamian and John Issa's Breezes, and is *en route* from downtown Nassau on the picturesque ride to Chris Blackwell's Compass Point.

Opposite page: Compass Point, a collection of 19 huts and cottages lies West of Cable Beach, *adjacent to the famous Love Beach.*

Top, left, the super-inclusive Breezes Resort.
Among the best hotel complexes in Cable Beach *are the Sandals Royal Bahamian Resort & Spa (right: top and center) and the Radisson Cable Beach Resort (below).*

PARADISE ISLAND and ATLANTIS

THE EARLY YEARS

Since time immemorial, mankind has been trying to regain Paradise. When the Swedish industrialist Dr. Axel Wenner-Gren docked his yacht in Nassau harbour in 1939, he had already travelled 70,000 miles and he hadn't yet found his paradise. Gazing on long lying Hog Island, as it was then called, with its ragged shrubs and trees, he must have heard a whisper of paradise from the cooling breeze which continously drifts across the island.

He bought the Lynch Estate, dredged a pond and renamed it Paradise Lake and that was the beginning of a chequered history, as the land passed from Gren to Huntington Hartford in 1961. It was he who changed the name to Paradise Island and began its transition into a modern resort with 1,000 hotel rooms and dozens of restaurants serving all kinds of international dishes.

One of the main attractions of Paradise Island was Saratoga Beach, which was renamed **Paradise Beach**.

The early years portrayed images of peace and complete relaxation on Paradise Island.

After crossing the bridge one would turn right at Paradise Island and drive to the heart of Hartford's dream. A shady driveway would take you to the steps of a pale pink Georgian style mansion called the Ocean Club Hotel. A doorman in livery would open the front door and sweep you into the entry hall.

Surrounding the hotel were Hartford's elegant **Versailles Gardens**, which appeared to be fresh from France if somewhat partially in the Hollywood style. Wenner-Gren, inspired by Louis XIV's gardens at Versailles, initiated the project and Hartford completed it. There were shady niches sheltering bronze statues – not of Venus or Apollo but of Livingstone and Roosevelt, both heroes of Hartford's world. There were also statues of Napoleon, Josephine, Hercules, and a bronze mother and child. From the garden's highest terrace one would cross Paradise Island and drive to the **cloisters**. An authentic medieval cloister which the Augustinian Friars had built in the middle of the XIVth century at Montréjeau, in France. After being taken to pieces stone by stone, the cloister was brought here and it took eccentric Randolph Hearst a year to rebuild it.

Two views of the French Cloister.

Opposite, top, an aerial view of the Ocean Club Hotel; bottom, the Club Med pool.

Paradise Island, Atlantis:

opposite page, the Royal Towers *and a view of the pool from above;*

this page, the Royal Towers *(detail), the* Casino, *the* Ruins Lagoon *and the* Great Hall of Waters *lobby.*

Atlantis in Paradise

Atlantis, Paradise Island, today, is not just a resort but a mythical land. It is a glorious celebration of the legends of the lost continent of Atlantis.

The $ 800 million resort completed in December 1998 is the world's largest island resort destination. It offers more than 2,300 guest accomodations, the most exciting **Carribean Casino**, 38 restaurants, bar and lounges, every kind of water activities, and attractions, including waterslides, waterfalls, 11 pool areas, and exhibit lagoons.

In Atlantis guests will find a spa, a fitness center, and an endless stretch of beach that has been defined the most beautiful in the world.

The **Royal Towers**, two twin towers with 1,202 accomodations, are the center of this fantastic resort. All around, guests are greeted by water cascading down to suggest that Atlantis has just risen from the

deep. Inside these marvellous towers the **Great Hall of Waters** lobby creates a memorable first impression.

But the main attraction of Atlantis is the largest marine habitat in the world, where over 150 species of exotic tropical fishes live in exhibit lagoons and displays, including **The Dig**, a maze of underwater corridors and passageways through the ancient civilization of Atlantis. Guests are fascinated by this underwater world where piranhas, rays, jellyfishes, and even sharks move silently. The resort also can claim the docking facility in the Bahamas: **Marina** at Atlantis, the luxury yacht harbour which is the destination for the finest vessels and offers a variety of further services.

Paradise Island, Atlantis:

opposite page, the Royal Towers *and a view of the beach;*

this page, the Mayan Temple, *dusk on the pool, the* Atlantis Aquarium, *another view of the beach.*

Following pages, an aerial view of the Blue Lagoon.

Grand Bahama

*T*his is the northernmost island of the archipelago and the closest to Florida, and in fact both its look and lifestyle are more American than Bahamian. In just a few years, the Grand Bahama has become much easier to reach than it used to be, when there were no signal beacons and, above all, ships did not have the sophisticated equipment which now makes it possible to individuate the low bottoms and the rocky shoals that in the past were often the cause of shipwrecks. Today, the Grand Bahama is the most-visited island after New Providence and Paradise Island, thanks also to its kilometres of enchanting beaches with modern hotels, gambling casinos, and diving clubs.

Between the modern and prestigious city of **Freeport** and the residential Lucaya is a small, uncontaminated paradise: the **Lucayan National Park**, with the most extensive system of caves known in all the world.

FREEPORT

*I*n just over a decade, a forest of scrub and pines has been converted into the second city of the Bahamas.

Freeport was the idea of Wallace Groves, a financier from Norfolk in Virginia. He sought and obtained a concession from the government with the assistance of Sir Stafford Sands, who was a lawyer and at the same time the Minister of Tourism.

Groves proposed to develop a free port on Grand Bahama. He asked for and received concessions to import duty free materials and guaranteed that there would be no taxes of any kind. In return he promised to dredge a deepwater harbour, encourage industry and pay for all the government personnel employed in the Port Area. This then became what is known as the Hawksbill Creek Agreement.

Five years later, seeing that business was good, Grove's company, the Grand Bahama Authority, sensing that the island's future lay more in tourism than industry, signed a supplemental agreement which turned it into tourism. In partnership with Louis Chesler, Groves built the Lucayan Beach Hotel, which incorporated a large gambling casino, the first of its kind on the Bahamas.

Freeport: *the splendid Princess Tower Hotel, in oriental style.*

A bright red colours the sea around Freeport *at sunset.*

Not far from the Lucayan Beach Hotel grew the famous **International Bazaar**, a curious architectural mélange designed in 1967 by a script-writer from Hollywood. It takes up over 40,000 square meters. The Bazaar covers the whole range of English, Scandinavian, Chinese, Japanese, Turkish, Indian, French, and Spanish architecture (to name a few countries), which in many cases succeed in capturing the atmosphere it was designed to create. In this enormous complex, which is almost a town within a town, one can buy all kinds of products from all over the world. Next to the International Bazaar is located the pharaonic **Princess Casino**, built in Moorish style: it looks as if it's the largest casino in the world.

On these pages, Freeport: some views of the International Bazaar, *where shops in Spanish, Chinese, Italian, and Indian styles offer tourist products from all over the world.*

In the Garden of the Groves *one can see elegant pink flamingoes walking by the side of a pond with waterfalls.*

GARDEN OF THE GROVES

The Garden of the Groves is a spectacular botanical garden designed from scratch; a gift from Wallace Groves to the island. It stretches over four hectares and contains a fine display of labelled exotic trees, plants, and shrubs from all over the world, with cascading waterfalls, flamingoes, and a gully of ferns. Complementing the garden is the **Grand Bahama Museum**, which captures the history of the island and features reconstructed caves and audio-visual presentations. There are also a marine exhibit and artifacts from the Lucayan Indian culture and the times of piracy.

In a small garden attached to the Museum is a native house reconstructed from local pine wood. Before leaving, note the driving wheels of a steam locomotive that was once used in the island's timber industry.

Freeport has centainly done its fair share in the participation of the rise and fall cycle that has been typical of the greater part of the Bahamian development, but it seems once again destined to rise to another economic boom.

Some examples of the magnificent flora which can be found in the Garden of the Groves.

FAMILY ISLANDS

*Also known by the name of **Out Islands**, the mysterious and exceptionally beautiful Family Islands, where time seems to have stopped, where one breathes the air of the Bahamas of old, are an uncontaminated environment pervaded by the scents of the famous local flowers, while the incredible variety of coral formations in crystal-clear waters are the natural habitat of many species of fish. And these seas are in fact one of the favourite destinations of* sailing and underwater sport enthusiasts as well as deep-sea fishermen. However, as the great number of wrecks on the sea bottom reminds us, it has always been difficult to reach these islands, due to the coral reefs and the sand banks. Above all for this reason, the inhabitants of the islands have, with time, become masterful boat builders and expert sailors. Today, these problems no longer exist, thanks to the scheduled flights that link the Bahamas to the rest of the world.

Bimini

Very close to Florida (so close in fact that it is said that on a clear night you can see the lights of Miami), Bimini is actually two larger islands, **North Bimini** and **South Bimini**, plus a chain of minor islands extending southward for about 45 kilometres. The most important city of North Bimini is **Alice Town**, not just because it boasts hotels, bars, and typical haunts, but also because the legendary **Ernest Hemingway** stayed here in far-off 1935. The legend narrates that when the writer heard about this island, he was so fascinated by the stories that he purchased a boat to try to reach it. During the long crossing, Hemingway spent his time fishing, and when he finally landed on the island the inhabitants were amazed by the number of fish the foreigner had managed to pull onboard. Hemingway was in fact later responsible for spreading the fame of these waters as an unparalleled fishing-ground - and Bimini still holds the prestigious title of the "world deep-sea fishing capital".

Fishing off Bimini.

Berry Islands

The **Berry Islands** are among the least-known of the Bahamas, and it is only rarely that cruise ships make brief stops to give tourists a close-up view of the natural beauty of this group of about thirty islands. In fact, this paradise has been almost entirely bought up by wealthy foreigners, who have made private hideaways of almost all of the islands. A number of these islands, or cays, can be visited by owners' invitation: **Bird Cay**, **Whale Cay**, **Frozen Cay**, and **Alder Cay** are among these. The latter two islands form a bird sanctuary, and one is crowded at sunset, when the sky fills with wheeling terns and pelicans, in a scintillating spectacle of flight. Some of the Berry Islands can be reached only by rowboat because of the dangerously shallow waters. The largest of the islands is **Great Harbour Cay**, where the population lives mainly by fishing and where tourist accommodations are still meagre. On the other hand, the smallest and southernmost island, **Chub Cay**, has always been organized for welcoming visitors.

Sunset in the Family Islands.

Abaco

ocated 170 kilometres north of Nassau, the **Abaco** group counts two large islands, **Great Abaco** and **Little Abaco**, and a myriad of small atolls around the "dry land". Communications among the islands are made difficult by the shallow waters, and it is perhaps for this reason that the inhabitants have become the most skilful boat-builders in the Bahamas. They have of course been helped along in their vocation by the raw materials provided by the pine forests that cover much of the surface of the islands. Boat-building has made these tiny, out-of-the-way islands and their inhabitants famous throughout the world.
Great Abaco, the larger of the two major islands, has many swamps that extend along the coast on the

Great Abaco, *Elbow Cay,* Hope Town *Harbour.*

Great Abaco, Marsh Harbour, *Sea View Castle Café.*

west side of the island; due to this natural feature, the "cities" have all grown up near the eastern coast. The commercial centre of Great Abaco is **Marsh Harbour**, with a great variety of modern food shops, many emporiums, banks, a few restaurants, a beauty salon, and gas stations. As to population density, Marsh Harbour is the third largest city in the Bahamas.
Easy to reach by sea from Marsh Harbour is **Hope Town**, a colourful village that is home to a famous and much-photographed red-and-white striped lighthouse, one of the few manned lighthouses still in operation. The village's past is today preserved in the *Wyami Malone Historical Museum.*
The adjacent Little Abaco is not as often visited by tourists. Among the smaller islands is the famous **Man-O-War Cay**, where like most everywhere in the Abaco group the main activity is boat-building. But the curious fact about it is that the inhabitants of the village, who are extremely proud of their traditions, are firmly opposed to tourist development.

Eleuthera, Harbour Island and Spanish Wells

Northeast of Nassau is the island of **Eleuthera**. The Greek name, which means "liberty", is itself an apt description of the carefree pause that this ancient land, with its glorious past and at the same time modern facilities, can offer the visitor. Eleuthera is characterized by a great variety of landscapes, surely, but also by a similar variety of ethnic groups: the first inhabitants were religious dissidents who left Bermuda 300 years ago in search of a homeland. The population later increased when the government of Bermuda dispatched slaves and free Africans to these islands, and it was again augmented by Loyalists fleeing America. The different cultures that populate this part of the world make a stay in these islands a special and unique experience.

The most important centre on Eleuthera is the by-now faded **Governor's Harbour**, which in its period of greatest prosperity was one of the most renowned cities of the Bahamas. **Rock Sound**, the other large city on Eleuthera, has all that's needed to make a stay on the island a pleasant experience for the many tourists who come here. A little more than one kilometre east of Rock Sound is the peerless *Rock Sound Ocean Hole*, a beautiful natural aquarium. To the northeast off the Eleuthera coast is **Harbour Island**, which was an important shipyard during World War II. **Dunmore Town**, the main settlement on the island, was in the 1800s the Bahama's second city both as to population and wealth, where vessels of every kind were built. With a fine natural harbour (hence the name), Harbour Island is today a small, peaceful community where the main activities are fishing and agriculture - and it is home, besides to many avant-garde tourist facilities, to the world-famous **Pink Sand Beach**. Further north is the minuscule **Spanish Wells**, an island about three kilometres long and one wide that distinguishes itself from the others due to the fact that its population has remained practically constant over the centuries. Spanish Wells is also the Bahamas' wealthiest community, thanks to the profitable lobster and giant sea bass fishing industries.

Eleuthera, Harbour Island, *horseback riding on Pink Beach.*

Eleuthera, Harbour Island, *clapboard house on Bay Street.*

Following pages: Family Islands, *panoramic view.*

Andros

T his largest island in the Bahamas, about 225 kilometres in length and 64 kilometres wide, lies west of Nassau. It is also one of the most populous. The western coast of Andros is inaccessible from the ocean because of the coral reef barrier, but tourists can easily reach the island by plane.

The barrier that makes Andros a much-visited attraction for diving enthusiasts divides the **Great Bahama Bank**, an area in which the water is never deeper than 3.5 metres, from the **Tongue of the Ocean**, a splendid abyss over 3000 metres deep and a true anomaly among the generally shallow waters of the Bahamas. The most important diving club is at *Small Hope Bay Lodge*.

Besides the barrier, in the crystalline waters of this splendid sea are also the milieu of the unusual **blue holes**, underwater springs of fresh water. When the water rises to the surface it forms peculiar dark blue blotches on the lighter surface of the sea.

But Andros' blue ribbons are not all for diving. It is also a well-known sport-fishing centre. What is more, the extensive nature preserves of the island are opened to hunters during certain periods of the year: one of the traditional preys is the white-crested pigeon.

Long Island

Long Island was baptized "Fernanda" by Christopher Columbus, and even earlier was called "Yuma" by the Arawakan Indians. Its administrative centre is **Clarence Town**; the symbols of the city are its two white churches, one with red decoration (St. Paul's Anglican Church), the other with blue (St. Peter's Catholic Church), built on two facing hills by the famous Father Jerome, an architect of proven expertise and the author of many buildings here and there throughout the Bahamas, like the small convent of Cat Island, the Hermitage, and the St. Augustine Monastery in Nassau. **Deadman's Cay**, much more populous than Clarence Town (over a third of the island's inhabitants live here), is the only "metropolis" on Long Island, from both the commercial and tourist points of view. Long Island is known above all for its annual regatta, held on Pentecost Monday at **Salt Pond**, attracting a multitude of sailing enthusiasts.

Cat Island

About eighty kilometres long, Cat Island owes its name to a pirate, a certain Arthur Catt, who used to rendezvous with his comrades here. The island, because it was a pirate cove, has always been surrounded by stories of mysterious hidden treasures and legends of ghosts. If one adds to this the fact that magic is a common practice here, a visit to Cat Island has always been a somewhat unsettling experience. For this reason it is one of the less popular tourist destinations and also one of the lesser-known islands of the archipelago.

Cat Island has a large lake and an immense bay called **The Bight**, which has on its shores two villages by the names of **New Bight** and **Old Bight**. In the latter, one can visit the *Pigeon Bay Cottage*, the remaining construction of the manor house complex of a vast cotton plantation built during the period in which cotton was the island's major product.

Another example of the splendour of times past is the *Deveaux House* of Port Howe, where in the early 1800s Georgia cotton was cultivated. Today, all that is visitable is the skeleton of the ancient plantation house. It is worthwhile making the effort to reach Mount Alvernia, the highest in the Bahamas (70 metres) where Father Jerome, an Anglican priest converted to Roman Catholicism, built his hermitage. He called the "peak" the "top of the world" because wherever one looks one sees the ocean. The *Hermitage*, as the small monastery was called, is accessible up a narrow path that from New Bight passes the Stations of the Cross set up by Father Jerome himself. Tourists can reach the island by air, landing at the field at Arthur's Town, where the actor Sidney Poitier was born, and lodge at Fernandez Bay Village, a small tourist centre.

San Salvador, *Cockburn Town.*

San Salvador

It was here, on 12 October 1492, that Christopher Colombus began his discovery of the New World. Once he sighted dry land, with the circumspection typical of the expert navigator, Columbus waited for dawn. In the daylight, he was able to see the coral barrier reef that surrounds the island, and sailed around it until he found a way in to a bay, today called **Long Bay**. Divers will find a bronze monument on the lagoon bottom at the point at which Columbus dropped anchor; a white cross on the shore marks the spot where he landed. The inhabitants met by Columbus lived in a village near the beach. Although it now no longer exists, excavations have revealed that the natives traded with Columbus' crew.
The **Riding Rocks,** on the north coast, are interesting formations that emerge and disappear again as the tide rises and falls. It is here that the most important of San Salvador's hotels is located: the Riding Rock Inn, near the easy-to-reach *panoramic tower* that offers a fine view of the entire island, with its small lakes and famous **Dixon Hill** lighthouse, which like that of Hope Town in the Abaco Islands is still manually operated.

The Exumas

This is a chain of small atolls, or *cays*, that runs for about 150 kilometres southeast of Nassau. The inhabitants are concentrated on the two largest islands, **Great Exuma** and **Little Exuma**, which are linked by a bridge over the Ferry Channel strait. George Town, the administrative centre of the Exumas, is distinguished by its pastel-coloured homes, the Elizabeth Harbour natural port, and St. Andrew's Anglican Church, built around 1850.
The area north of George Town is also interesting, with its many small farms and further on a beautiful, long, deserted beach called **Jimmy Hill**. South of George Town, across the bridge that connects Great Exuma and Little Exuma, is **Pretty Molly Bay**, of which it is said that at full moon one can see a beautiful siren seated on the rocks combing her long hair. These small islands, however, are world-famous for another reason: the Bahamian iguana, a protected species that can be seen at *Exuma Cay Land and Sea Park*, a beautiful maritime and terrestrial nature preserve.
Sailing enthusiasts come every year to the Exumas for the famous three-day regatta held here.

SOUTHERN ISLANDS

These are the southernmost of the Out Islands, the most difficult to reach (only by private boat or with the mail boats), and the least known. The hotels and restaurants are few, but these islands are nevertheless a paradise for those seeking respite from the daily stress of city life and asking for nothing more than peace and quite in contact with nature, which here is uniquely enchanting to say the least.

The most important of the southern islands is **Great Inagua**, commonly known simply as Inagua, located at the extreme southern tip of the chain. It is the peak of an underwater mountain, and is the third largest island in the entire Bahamian archipelago as to surface area. Inagua is famous throughout the world for the pink flamingoes of the Bahamas, which in times past populated the entire island and in particular the **Lake Rosa** area. These splendid birds were mercilessly hunted until becoming a rarity. Today, the *Inagua National Park* nature preserve covers 50% of the island, and it is here that every spring the surviving flamingoes, which have become the symbols of the Bahamas, return to populate their ancient summer home.

North of Inagua is **Little Inagua**, a deserted, wild island protected by deep waters and hosting the only spontaneous Royal Palm wood in the Bahamas. North of Little Inagua is the medium-sized island of **Mayaguana**. The 600 people that live here live almost all in the administrative centre, **Abraham's Bay**. Mayaguana is one of the few islands of the Bahamas to have preserved its ancient Indian name; and life too is as simple as it once was.

On **Crooked Island**, a sparsely-populated island given over mostly to agriculture, don't miss the *Marine Farm*, located at the northwestern tip. Besides the *Hope Great House*, it is the only old cotton plantation-house still standing in the Bahamas. It dominates the Crooked Island Passage, a deep channel separating the central Bahamas from the southern islands.

A lagoon called the *Bight of Acklins* separates Crooked Island from the other southern island, **Acklins**.

Recent discoveries have revealed that Acklins Island, which was baptized "Isabella" by Columbus, probably hosted the largest native community in the Bahamas.

Pink Flamingoes.

GOLF COURSES

he Bahamas are also about walking on the greens and carrying a stick, and indeed they host several leading international golf tournaments. Some of the best golfing in the islands is found in Nassau. The Cable Beach Golf Club is the oldest golf course, a spectacular 18-hole, well maintained fairways dotted with water traps, and extremely fast. The Paradise Island Golf Club, designed by Dick Wilson, featuring over 80 sand traps, windmill, and water pipe, is also known for its rippling greens, while its 14th hole offers magnificent vistas of the Atlantic Ocean. Yet the most challenging golf course remains the South Ocean Golf Course, with some first-rate holes with a backdrop of trees, bushes and ondulating hills.

One can say that both Nassau and Paradise Island are ideal for those fond of golf: the Radisson Cable Beach Golf Club is one of the oldest (it was opened in 1926).
The Paradise Island Golf Course (below) boasts the worlds most beautiful "water trap".

FLORA

The archipelago of the Bahamas is made up of rather flat islands with indented coastlines; for this reason, the prevalent type of habitat is coastal, and hosts a widely-diversified flora of great visual impact. Among the dominant species along the coasts, the first the visitor is likely to encounter is *cocos nucifera*, the *coconut palm*, which is found in both the wildest and the most built-up parts of the Bahamas. Often, in the shade of the crowns of the coconut palms, one will see the *bay hop*, a ground-creeper that is easy to recognize thanks to its large purplish flowers that in the morning emanate an intense scent that attracts pollinating insects. In the sandy and the rocky coastal habitats, the *seaside lavender* and the *seaside ox-eye* are common. The *sea grape* instead marks the passage from

1. **Coconut palm** *(cocos nucifera)*
2. **Bay hop** *(ipomoea pes-caprae)*
3. **Seaside lavender** *(argusia gnaphaloides)*

1

2

3

the dry, sandy or rocky coasts to the brackish marsh environments dominated by the mangrove forests. In these habitats, the *red mangrove* (*rhizophora mangle*) prevails in the wettest areas and the *bottom wood* (*conocarpus erectus*) where the land is drier. There is also a form of the later species with sericeous leaves that is sometimes referred to as *c. sericeus* Forssk. In the coastal pine woods one will find the *purple bletia*, while the forests are populated by various species of trees and shrubs, among which the *beef bush* (found only on New Providence and Andros), the *ram-goat dashalong*, the *red cordia*, and the *yellow elder*, the official flower of the Bahamas.

4. *Seaside ox-eye* (*borrichia arborescens*)
5. *Sea grape* (*coccoloba uvifera*)
6. *Red mangrove* (*rhizophora mangle*)
7. *Bottom wood* (*conocarpus erectus*)
8. *Purple bletia* (*bletia purpurea*)
9. *Beef bush* (*tabebuia bahamensis*)
10. *Ram-goat dashalong* (*turnera ulmifolia*)
11. *Red cordia* (*cordia sebestena*)
12. *Yellow elder* (*tecoma stans*)

4

5

6

9

10

7

11

8

12

THE BAHAMAS: A DIVERS' PARADISE

1

The water here is so transparent that equipment is rarely needed to admire the marvels of the innumerable coral barriers. A true paradise for divers, with millions of tropical fish and other ocean-dwellers, and many centuries-old wrecks, victims of the sand banks. But even those who only go snorkeling will be amazed at the enormous variety of corals and barrier fish found in just a few meters of sea. All the Bahamas tourist operators offer professional assistance and most are members of the Bahamas Diving Association (BDA). Strangely enough, although the Bahamas are visited by nearly 100,000 divers a year, it is rare to encounter another diving boat out on the water. The reason? Simply the enormity of the territory. Where to dive? If your interest is generic, you may want to stay close to Nassau, with its coral barrier and wrecks. If your passion is instead flying down a drop-off, few places are better than the world-famous San Salvador, Conception Island, or Salt Cay, or the legendary **Tongue of the Ocean**, with its 2000-meter walls off the south and west of New Providence or the east coast of Andros. Any island of the Bahama bank will do for shallow waters and barriers abounding in schools of fish and invertebrates, but Exuma, Bimini, Long Island, and Eleuthera excel. **"Blue holes"** and grottoes are the pride of Andros and Grand Bahama. The reef enclosing the shallow waters off Abaco is a maze of intertwining grottoes. Sharks are the order of the day at Grand Bahama, New Providence, Walker's Cay, and Long Island. Dolphins? Try **White Sand Ridge**, north of Grand Bahama, where expert UNEXSO guides attract their attention.

1. *Leopard Moray.*

2. *Pork Fish, and Orange Sponge.*

3. *Diver with a Grouper.*

4. *Two of Sea Anemones.*

5. *Queen Angelfish.*

2

3

4

5

INDEX

PHOTOGRAPHY ACKNOWLEDGMENTS

The photographs belong to the Archives of the Casa Editrice Bonechi *except those on the following pages:*

Page 57: Brett Froomen/ The Image Bank
Pages 59, 60, 61: Andrea Innocenti
Pages 17 bottom, 34, 35, 37 bottom, 45, 54/55, 62, 63: Leonardo Olmi
Pages 8, 9, 36 top, 37 top, 39 top (right), 40 bottom, 41 right (top, centre and bottom), 42/43: Andrea Pistolesi
Pages 7, 11, 14 bottom, 15, 17 top, 18 bottom, 20, 32, 33, 38, 39 top (left), centre and bottom, 40 top, 41 left, 51 centre, 52, 53, 56, 58 bottom:
photos kindly supplied by LMH Publishing Ltd *and* Bahamas Tourist Board.